Piers of Disaster

The Sad Story of the Seaside Pleasure Piers of the Yorkshire Coast

by Martin Easdown

Hutton Press
1996

Published by

The Hutton Press Ltd.,
130 Canada Drive, Cherry Burton,
Beverley, East Yorkshire HU17 7SB.

Printed by
Image Colourprint Ltd.,
Willerby, Hull.

ISBN 1 872167 81 0

CONTENTS

ACKNOWLEDGEMENTS

The Author wishes to thank the following for permission to reproduce their illustrations:-

Norman Bainbridge - Pages 14, 15 (top), 17, 18, 20 (bottom), 21 (bottom), 22 (top).
Langbaurgh-on-Tees Borough Council - Pages 15 (bottom), 16 (bottom), 20 (top), 21 (top), 22 (bottom).
Valentines of Dundee - Page 19 (bottom).
Daphne Leach - Pages 23, 44 (bottom).
North Yorkshire County Libraries - Page 26 (top).
Kirkleatham Old Hall Museum, Redcar - Pages 38 (top), 41 (bottom).
Beamish Open Air Museum - Page 41 (top).
Cleveland County Libraries - Pages 42, 43 (top).
John Whitehead (Reprinted from his book 'Withernsea' by Highgate Publications) - Page 47 (top).
David Cookson - Page 47 (bottom).
Frank Hobson - Pages 48 (top), 52 (bottom), 55 (bottom), 57, 58.
Jack Whittaker - Pages 48 (bottom), 49 (bottom).
Hornsea Museum - Pages 55 (bottom), 56.

All other illustrations are from the author's own collection.

A special thanks must be made to John Whitehead and David Cookson for their information on Withernsea Pier, Frank Hobson for Hornsea Pier and Norman Bainbridge for Saltburn Pier. Thank you also to Chris Ketchell at Hull College for Further Education, East Yorkshire Libraries (Beverley Group Headquarters), Redcar Library, The National Piers Society, Mrs Jean Smith, Mrs Margaret Bowers for the original typesetting, Rev. Peter Bowers and of course my wife, Jackie and children Tom, Sarah and Bethany for putting up with my endless conversations about Piers!

In memory of Robert Eastleigh.

INTRODUCTION

Visitors to the small seaside resort of Withernsea on the Holderness coast of Yorkshire, must often stare in amazement at the castle-like building situated on the promenade and wonder why it was ever built. Many of them probably regard it as some kind of seaside 'folly', unaware that it was once the entrance building to a pier that disappeared a long time ago.

Withernsea pier was one of six seaside pleasure piers that once graced the Yorkshire coastline, but today only one of them, Saltburn, still survives and that is now less than half its original length.

The story of Yorkshire's seaside pleasure piers, and why they disappeared is a sad, but often a fascinating one.

Saltburn Pier. RELIABLE SERIES. R1658

Saltburn Pier in 1899. This was the first pleasure pier to be sanctioned in Yorkshire and is the only surviving pier today.

THE OLD CHAIN PIER BRIGHTON.
BUILT 1823. DESTROYED DEC·4·1896.

The Chain Pier, Brighton was one of the earliest and most famous pleasure piers to be constructed. It was later destroyed by a storm in December 1896.

THE BIRTH OF THE SEASIDE RESORT AND THE PLEASURE PIER

The birth of the seaside resort began in the first half of the eighteenth Century, when Sir John Floyer and Dr Richard Russell expounded the virtues of drinking seawater to cure all manner of illnesses, including rheumatism, cancer, hernias, deafness, ulcers and consumption, just to name a few! Doctors and Physicians of the time soon encouraged this practice, along with the breathing in of the ozone in the sea air, and by the beginning of the nineteenth century, former fishing villages like Brighton and Margate, and the Spa town of Scarborough, were amongst the first coastal towns to develop as fashionable 'watering places'. Those who had previously regarded the sea with some suspicion now flocked to it, forsaking the old inland Spa towns which had previously catered for their ills.

Steam passenger boats enabled the middle and upper classes to travel in relative comfort to these resorts, though to disembark from the boats to land on the shore often meant an uncomfortable journey in a small leaky rowing boat or on the back of some burly local fisherman! Some of the stone harbour protection piers were used as landing stages, but they were often unsuitable and on occasions they damaged the boats.

In 1814 Ryde, on the Isle of Wight, became one of the earliest resorts to build a piled wooden landing pier and nine years later, the famous chain pier at Brighton was opened, which soon acquired a reputation as a fashionable promenade rather than just as a landing pier. Further piers were built between 1830 and 1858, but it was not until the 1860's, when some twenty piers were constructed, that 'Pier Mania' began. By this time, the rapidly expanding railway network had vastly improved inland transport to these rising 'Watering Places' and

this coupled with the various Factory Acts had enabled even a few of the working class to have a day out at the seaside.

Another factor in the growth of the seaside pier was the use of iron in their construction, which along with improved methods of securing and supporting piles into the beach, gave them a greater stability and made them easier to construct.

Southport Pier, opened in 1860 and constructed of iron, was one of the first piers to be built primarily for use as a promenade rather than just a landing stage. It is sometimes known as the 'first true pleasure pier'.

Admission onto these early piers was not cheap, but for your money you got an unrivalled view of the town, a chance to breath in all that health-giving sea air and the feeling of being on the sea without having to worry about feeling sea-sick. There were also refreshment and reading rooms, and bandstands on some piers.

Many Company promoters and investors now viewed that a pleasure pier was an essential addition to their resort, if they were to attract the ever increasing numbers of visitors to the sea. The increased availability of a limited liability for shareholders prompted local residents from the resorts to invest in shares in the local pier company, no doubt hoping for a healthy dividend. Not all piers were to be a success though, and many shareholders, especially in the small resorts, never received a penny on their investments.

In the next fifty years or so, between 1860 and 1910, some ninety seaside pleasure piers were built around the coasts of Great Britain and the Isle of Man, with varying degrees of success. Many piers later acquired opulent moorish and oriental styled pavilions, along with other forms of amusement. A few hours on the pier listening to the band, watching a show in the pavilion, fishing or just taking a casual stroll became an integral part of the British seaside holiday.

Central Pier, Blackpool

Above Left: Southport Pier was built in 1860, at the start of the golden age of pier building, which was to last fifty years.

Left: The Central Pier, Blackpool c1890, was one of a number of successful piers, which graced the Lancashire coastline.

A BACKGROUND TO THE SEASIDE PLEASURE PIERS OF YORKSHIRE

Yorkshire's long coastline was in the forefront of the pier building era, when a pier was planned for Saltburn as early as 1861. It was eventually opened in 1869 followed in turn by piers at Scarborough (1869), Redcar (1873), Coatham (1875), Withernsea (1878) and Hornsea (1880). Unfortunately their impact was to be far less marked than many other piers around the country and by 1910 four of them had been demolished. There were a number of reasons why this was so.

Scarborough was the only major resort on the Yorkshire coast to acquire a pleasure pier. Filey, Whitby and Bridlington did without them (though the latter two resorts had stone harbour piers which were used for promenading); while the five remaining resorts were speculative places with rather limited appeal. The building of a pier was seen as a major stepping stone in their quest to become the next 'Scarborough' or 'Brighton', but development remained small, and the pier companies struggled to keep their heads above water as constant setbacks and misfortunes caused debts to mount up.

Across the Pennines in Lancashire on the other hand, business in the coastal resorts was booming. By 1875, there were two piers at Blackpool, the pioneering working class resort, and one each at Morecambe, Southport and Lytham, plus another just across the Mersey in Cheshire at New Brighton. To the detriment of the Yorkshire resorts, the great industrial towns of the West Riding tended to encamp on mass to their Lancashire counterparts for their holiday weeks. Morecambe became so popular with folk from Yorkshire, it was nicknamed 'Bradford-on-Sea'.

Nature's twin forces of wind and tide were undoubtedly the major factors though in the disappearance of the Yorkshire piers.

Scarborough Pier was almost completely washed away in a bad storm in January 1905 and it was never rebuilt. Three of its contemporaries were irrevocably damaged by sail-driven ships, which were difficult to control in bad weather.

Hornsea Pier had only been opened for five months, when in 1880 a storm-damaged vessel hit the pier destroying the pierhead and 120ft of the neck. The pier company, already in severe financial trouble, simply could not afford to repair the pier, which was left to rot away.

Withernsea Pier seemed to have magnetic attraction for storm-damaged vessels, which regularly smashed into the pier until there was virtually nothing left of it.

Coatham Pier was a fairly impressive structure, but it was just too close to its neighbour at Redcar to ever be profitable. The twin towns were simply not popular enough to support two piers, so when Coatham Pier was cut in two by ship collision in 1898, the pier company went bankrupt and the pier was demolished for scrap.

Its rival at Redcar, on the other hand, managed to survive into the twentieth century where its pavilion became a popular attraction for many varied entertainments until the pier's demolition in 1981.

The last surviving Yorkshire pier, Saltburn, was almost demolished in 1974 following a catalogue of disasters, and it was only saved after a public enquiry recommended the partial demolition of the seaward end. In 1978, the pier was restored and re-opened to the public, and at the present time is still defying the fury of the North Sea after well over a hundred and twenty years of a near continuous pounding by it.

If the local authority continues to maintain and repair the pier on a regular basis, the story of Yorkshire's seaside pleasure piers could well continue into the twenty-first century. Not until Saltburn Pier has finally disappeared, will the story come to an end.

The Piers that follow are listed in chronological order of building.

The South Pier, Bridlington was a stone harbour pier which doubled up as a promenade. Bridlington never did acquire a pleasure pier.

SALTBURN PIER: 1869

The small seaside town of Saltburn-by-the-Sea was a creation of Henry Pease and the Saltburn Improvement Company during the middle of the nineteenth century. In the following years it grew slowly and unspectacularly into a popular family resort, much frequented by day visitors from Industrial Teeside.

Saltburn's attractive cast-iron pier, one of the earliest developments in the town, is now the last survivor of the six pleasure piers which once graced the Yorkshire coastline.

The origins of the pier go back to the beginning of the pier building era, when in 1861 work was sanctioned under the Piers and Harbours Act. Finance was to have been provided by the Saltburn Improvement Company, but nothing was done until the formation of the Saltburn Pier Company in October 1867. Resident Saltburn Engineer, John Anderson, was appointed as both Engineer and Contractor for the building of the pier, and in December 1867, the first consignment of ironwork was delivered by Cochrane and Grove of Ormesby Foundry. The first pile was driven in by Mrs Thomas Vaughan of Gunnergate Hall on the 27th January 1868, and seventeen months later, in May 1869, the pier was opened to the public.

Saltburn Pier was a conventional structure of the time, consisting of cast-iron piles supporting trestles of cast-iron beams which supported the wooden decking. It was 1,500 ft long and 20ft wide, with a landing stage at the pierhead, which could be used by both pleasure steamers and light craft. Two handsome octagonal kiosks were provided at the pier entrance for use as tollhouses. Facilities on the pier included a saloon on the pierhead and six small refreshment booths near the centre of the pier. Advertising space on the pierhead could be bought for 5/- per annum.

The pier was immediately successful, with over 50,000 people paying to use it in the first six months of its life. Pleasure Steamers running from Hartlepool to Whitby, Scarborough and Bridlington, called at the landing stage in the summer season, and they proved to be a popular attraction.

In 1870, the Saltburn Pier Company paid a 10% dividend to shareholders, and on a high hope of expectation they opened a 120ft high wooden vertical hoist opposite the pier entrance in July of the same year, to convey passengers up and down the cliffside. A walk along the high narrow gangway to the hoist however, was not one for the fainthearted!

The pier continued to make a profit in the following three years, but in 1873 the dividend paid out was only 1.25% and £2,500 was needed for improvements. Before these could be carried out, though, a storm in October 1875 completely wrecked the landing stage and the end of the pier. With no money left in its own coffers to pay for repairs, the pier company had to borrow £300 at 4% interest from the Saltburn Improvement Company.

In 1877 the pier was re-opened with a reduced length of 1,250 ft after being strengthened, and in that year the company paid a 1% dividend to its shareholders. However, by 1879, the Saltburn Pier Company had gone into liquidation due to mounting debts, and on the 30th August 1883 the pier became the property of the Saltburn

Improvement Company (who themselves were taken over by the Owners of the Middlesbrough Estates).

The new owners of the pier immediately made improvements. Before the end of 1883, a bandstand with seating protected by glass screens had been erected on an enlarged pierhead, and in the following year, an incline tramway was built to replace the dilapidated hoist. On the 20th July 1887 the pier became illuminated by electric light, and sometime during this period, the original entrance kiosks were replaced by two larger rectangular buildings in matching style with the cliff tramway building.

For the next thirty years or so, the pier led a relatively trouble-free life, in stark contrast to its five neighbours on the Yorkshire coast which were suffering all sorts of disasters. Fishing, band concerts and promenading were a popular feature of the pier, which was the major attraction in the resort.

Disaster struck however, on the 7th/8th May 1924 when the China Clay Vessel 'Ovenbeg' (formerly the Russian registered 'St.Nicholi') carrying a cargo of china from Fowey in Cornwall to Grangemouth was driven ashore just west of the pier during a strong gale. The weather moderated during the day and it was hoped to refloat the stricken vessel, but gales blew up again at nightfall, and they repeatedly smashed the 'Ovenbeg' against the seaward end of the pier until it broke through causing a 210 ft gap. The 'Ovenbeg' was eventually washed up onto the beach, a mangled wreck.

A barrier was erected by the Owners of the Saltburn Estates (a subsidiary of the Owners of the Middlesbrough Estates) at the end of the shortened pier, which enabled the rest of the structure to still be used for promenading. To compensate for the loss of the isolated pierhead bandstand, a small theatre building was erected at the pier entrance between the two tollhouses.

The pierhead bandstand and shelters were to remain isolated until 1930, when the gap in the pier was repaired using steel instead of the original cast-iron.

In 1938, the pier changed hands again, when it was purchased for only £12,000 by Saltburn and Marske Urban District Council under a special Act of Parliament. Two years later, though, it was requisitioned by the army and a 120 ft section of the pier near the promenade was removed to prevent it being used by the enemy in case of invasion.

The end of the war saw the pier in poor condition, and after much wrangling between the Council and Government Departments, it was repaired in 1947 at a cost of £20,000. Eventually in April 1952 the pier was re-opened to the public, and over 25,000 people used it during that first month. However, within a year, the pier had to closed again after gales had badly twisted the main structure, and repairs were not completed until 1958 after a further expenditure of £23,000.

Despite all these troubles, the pier was still a popular attraction and up to 90,000 people a year continued to use it. Fishing from the seaward end was the main source of income, though the café at the pier entrance was also popular.

The beginning of the 1970's however, saw the pier giving further cause for concern. In the Autumn of 1971, one of the supporting piles on the seaward end was lost, and though it was replaced the following year, a consultant engineer's report stated 'The general appearance of the pier is unfortunately marred by the extensive rusting of much of the steel and ironwork forming the main structure. However, it has plenty of reserve strength, enabling it to stand safely when some members are heavily corroded or missing. It has in the past survived the loss of a pile with no apparent ill effect'. An underwater survey confirmed that many of the supporting piles (especially the 1930 steel section) were in a poor condition, and in January 1973 the pier was declared not safe to use except in calm weather.

In June 1973, a pile was lost on the west side of the pierhead, and in the following November, the loss of a further pile on the eastern side of the pierhead saw the pier closed altogether. Two months later, the situation worsened, when three further piles were lost in a storm. The Borough and County Councils drew up an interim plan to provide emergency repairs at a cost of £40,000, but before this could come into effect, a severe storm on the 29th October 1974 washed away the pierhead and badly damaged the rest of the pier, thus reducing its length to 1,100 ft.

By now Langbaurgh Borough Council (who took over the pier following the local government re-organisations of 1974), had had enough, and in 1975 they applied to the Department of Environment for permission to demolish the pier (this was necessary as the pier was a listed building). An action group chaired by Langbaurgh Councillor, Mrs Audrey Collins, forced a public enquiry which was held over three days in November 1975. This recommended that only the thirteen end trestles of the pier be demolished, and the recommendations were taken up by Peter Shore, Secretary of State for the Environment, who refused Langbaurgh Borough Council permission to demolish the pier.

So in September 1976 restoration work began with the end trestles being demolished at a cost of £18,500. The remaining 681 ft of the pier was completely refurbished at a cost of £52,500 and on the 29th June 1978, the pier was re-opened to the public for the first time in nearly five years. In the following year, the buildings at the pier entrance were restored and re-opened as an amusement arcade and café.

Since then, the Tourism and Leisure Committee of Langbaurgh Borough Council have pledged a phased programme of restoration and maintenance for the pier, which has recently survived some rough handling by the weather without too much ill-effect.

Saltburn Pier has had probably the must turbulent history of any surviving seaside pleasure pier in Britain today, and it is a tribute to John Anderson that part of this gallant old structure is still with us. Long may she continue to provide relaxation and entertainment to people for many years to come.

Left: Saltburn Pier, in its original condition c1869. The short-lived landing stage, with two steamers calling, can be seen at the end of the 1,500ft long pier.

Below: Storm damage in 1875 destroyed the landing stage and seaward end of Saltburn Pier. In 1877 the pier was rebuilt to a shorter length of 1,250ft as seen in this photograph of the mid 1880s.

A close-up view of the bandstand and sheltered seating on the rebuilt pierhead of Saltburn Pier c1900. This was built at a higher level than the original pier, to which it is connected by a ramp.

Saltburn Pier during the Edwardian period. The original tollbooths have been replaced by two larger rectangular buildings constructed on a widened pier entrance, which housed a restaurant and shops.

Above: An on-the-deck view of Saltburn Pier from the pier head bandstand in about 1903.

Right: The seaward end of Saltburn Pier c1910. A few remains of the landing stage can be seen to the left of the pierhead.

Left: The storm damaged Schooner 'Ovenbeg' lies stricken and damaged, just West of Saltburn Pier, 7th May 1924

Below: On the following day, 8th May 1924, another storm drove the 'Ovenbeg' through the seaward end of Saltburn Pier, isolating the pierhead. The wrecked schooner lies smashed to pieces on the beach, surrounded by curious onlookers.

The pierhead bandstand of Saltburn Pier was to remain isolated for six years, until the pier was finally repaired in 1930. During this time, the shortened pier continued to be in use.

ZC.16 "CREAMING WAVES"
THE PIER. SALTBURN BY THE SEA

Left: Saltburn Pier in 1931, now fully restored following the 'Ovenbeg' disaster seven years previously. The new building at the pier entrance was constructed in 1925 for use as a theatre.

Below: A busy day on Saltburn beach, shortly after the pier was re-opened to the public in 1952, following damage sustained in the Second World War. The 1925 theatre building has been shortened to the same length as the other two entrance buildings and it has been converted into an amusement arcade.

Above: Saltburn Pier in 1974, unsafe and closed to the public due to the loss of some of the supporting piles over the previous year.

Right: This photograph was taken during the storm of October 29th 1974, just moments after the collapse of the pierhead into the sea.

*Above: The damaged seaward end of
Saltburn Pier following the storm of
October 29th 1974. Langbaurgh
Borough Council now wanted to
demolish the pier, but a public
enquiry held in November 1975
recommended the demolition of
only the thirteen end trestles.*

*Left: Demolition of the thirteen end
trestles of Saltburn Pier commenced in
September 1976, with work being
completed shortly afterwards.*

*Above: A new pierhead was then
constructed during 1977 onto the
refurbished section of Saltburn Pier,
giving it a new length of 681ft.*

*Right: On the 29th June 1978,
Saltburn Pier was opened to the public
for the first time in nearly five years.
The buildings at the pier entrance
were restored and re-opened in the
following year.*

Above: Saltburn Pier in October 1988. Despite all its troubles, the pier is still one of the most attractive structures of its kind in Great Britain.

Right: Saltburn from the end of the pier in October 1988. This quiet resort remains virtually unchanged since its foundation and growth during the Victorian and Edwardian eras.

SCARBOROUGH NORTH PIER:1869

The Ancient and historic town of Scarborough has the distinction of being one of the earliest coastal towns to develop into a seaside resort.

In 1626 a local lady, Mrs Elizabeth Farrer, discovered a natural spring, and its health-giving properties soon attracted a pilgrimage of wealthy people to this new Spa. While they were in town, they could also bathe in the sea and be cured of all manner of illnesses according to the eminent doctors of the day! This double attraction soon gave Scarborough a distinct advantage over many rival Spa towns and coastal resorts, and the development of the town proceeded rapidly in the early part of the nineteenth Century. In 1804 the bathing infirmary was opened and in 1826 the Cliff bridge was built, which allowed easy access to the town with its newly-built elegant terraces and crescents containing grand hotels and boarding houses. By the 1850's the railway had arrived and Thomas Cook's railway excursions brought train-loads of Midlanders to sample the sea air and sands.

Scarborough developed basically into a resort of two parts. The South Bay was the most popular part of the resort and the majority of the hotels and other seaside facilities were situated there. The North Bay by comparison was almost devoid of any facilities, and there was no made-up road giving easy access. It often seemed a lonely and windswept place, but this is where Scarborough's promenade pier was eventually built.

The first proposal to build a pier in Scarborough came in 1864, when a syndicate of Manchester businessmen sought to erect the pier close to the harbour in the South Bay, but this scheme failed due to the combined efforts of the local opposition and the Board of Trade, who decided the pier would be a hazard to navigation and shipping in general.

The man behind the eventual building of Scarborough's promenade pier was J.W.Woodall, a local banker, who formed a public limited company in 1865 with the intention of erecting a 1,000 ft pier in the North Bay. The prolific pier designer Eugenius Birch was engaged as the engineer and one of his regular contractors, J.E.Dowson, was to construct the pier. On the 14th September 1866, the first pile was driven into the beach and completion time for building the pier was expected to be around fifteen months. However, eighteen months later the pier was still unfinished, 200 ft short of its ultimate 1,000 ft. The delay was due to the death of Dowson, but eventually a new firm Head Wrightson & Co. of Stockton (who were to become one of the most famous and prolific of all pier builders) completed the structure.

On the first day of May 1869, the pier was finally opened to the public after having cost £12,135 to build. Entrance fees were 1d. for a casual stroll and ten shillings for a yearly permit for anglers. There was a small shelter on the pierhead, where band concerts and refreshments were provided, and continuous seating ran along both sides of the pier decking.

The Scarborough Promenade Pier Company Limited launched hopefully into their first season, but only small dividends of 1.5% and 2% were paid to shareholders in the early years. Further attractions to entice more visitors were out of the question as the pier company owed over £2,000 to local banks, and in the winter rough seas and storm damage soon caused inroads into what little money the company had. It was hoped the permission given for steamers to call at the pierhead would attract more visitors and bring in extra revenue, but the heavy seas caused the steamers to repeatedly damage the pier and they were reluctantly forbidden to call.

By 1879, the pier company was no longer paying a dividend, despite increased admission charges, and it was in serious financial trouble. In 1881, the sum of £375 was paid for repairs when one of the supporting piles gave way, but worse followed in 1883, when the steam trawler 'Star' ran into the pier demolishing some of the piles. Three weeks later, the steamer 'Hardwick' did the same thing and in December of the same year, a severe storm blew the band shelter clean off the pierhead. The pier was left unrepaired for a year or two, and annual receipts plummeted to just £200. Further damage occurred to the pier when the yacht 'Escalpa' crashed through it one winter's night.

Things went from bad to worse, and in 1888 receipts from the pier amounted to only £80, the lowest total by a large margin. The same year saw the cliff tramway opposite the pier entrance close down after a short life of only nine years, and these events convinced J.W.Woodall to wind up the pier company. Scarborough Corporation, who were starting on improvements to the North Bay, declined to buy the pier, but eventually it was purchased by Walter Hudson of London for £1,240. He formed the North Pier Company and they spent £10,000 on repairs and improvements to the pier, including enlarging the pierhead and erecting a pavilion on it. The original toll booths at the pier entrance were swept away and replaced by an attractive building incorporating a restaurant. These improvements, along with the newly-built Royal Albert Drive giving easy access, should have given the pier a new lease of life, but it still proved to be something of a 'white elephant', and even the variety shows laid on at the pierhead pavilion featuring famous artists Will Catlin and Marie Lloyd, failed to make the pier pay.

The last owner of Scarborough Pier was the Mayor of the day, William Morgan, who acquired it for £3,500 in 1904. He had speculated with success on the Aquarium and he had previous managerial experience in the entertainment world, but this time he was unlucky.

On the night of Friday 6th January, 1905, a north-west gale was blowing, causing heavy seas and an exceptionally high tide. The full force of the sea blasted into the North Bay and helped by the backwash from the Royal Albert Drive, the wind and waves effectively laid the whole pier in complete ruin. Only the pierhead pavilion at the seaward end remained standing, and this was left isolated beyond the low-water mark. Picture postcards showing the ruined pier were quickly printed and they were soon sold out, extra supplies having to be provided to meet the demand for them.

The pier was not covered by insurance and so it was never replaced. The isolated pierhead pavilion was soon demolished, though the entrance building of 1889 survived until 1914. A local paper commented at the time, 'The passing of Scarborough Pier has left the sea to be free once again to lash itself in fury against the Royal Albert Drive wall; washing gleefully over the foundations of what once had to meet the full force of the oncoming waves and was, to all intents and purposes, destroyed for daring to offer resistance'.

Above: Scarborough Pier in the late 1870s as originally built, with the small pierhead building and two entrance kiosks.

Left: Scarborough Pier changed hands in 1889 and new buildings were constructed on the pierhead and at the pier entrance, but still the pier proved to be unprofitable.

The seaward end of Scarborough Pier, seen from the Clarence Gardens c1895.

Scarborough Pier enduring a battering by the rough seas, which were soon to destroy it. c1898.

PROMENADE PIER, SCARBOROUGH.

Above: A calmer view of the North Bay, Scarborough c1900, showing the pier and in the background, the castle and the short-lived Warwick Revolving Tower (1898-1907).

Left: The entrance building of Scarborough Pier c1903, which housed a restaurant and shops.

Above: On 7th January 1905, Scarborough Pier was almost totally destroyed in a storm. This postcard shows the pier before and after the devastating storm.

Left: Amazingly, this postcard of the wrecked Scarborough Pier was photographed, printed, sold and posted within two days of the pier being destroyed! The sender of the card has written "This is the pier which was blown down on Saturday night. Rather sad, isn't it? You see the pavilion was saved, all the middle was broken away."

Promenade Pier—Scarborough. Before and after the Storm Jan. 7th. 1905.

Left: Another 'before and after' postcard view of Scarborough Pier, following the storm of the 7th January 1905.

Below: The isolated pierhead pavilion of Scarborough Pier lay stranded in the North Bay for a few months, until it was eventually dismantled.

The former entrance building of Scarborough Pier continued in use as
a restaurant and gift shop until its demolition in 1914.

REDCAR PIER : 1873

Redcar's development into a seaside resort began in the 1850's when its streets were cleared of sand and the whole town was generally smartened up. A sea wall and promenade were constructed in the 1860's and the next logical step for any developing resort in Victorian times was the erection of a promenade pier.

The Redcar Pier Company was formed in 1866 with the intention of providing Redcar with a 'commodious promenade and landing pier'. Parliamentary assent to build the pier was obtained shortly afterwards. Nothing was done, however, until 1870 when a rival scheme for neighbouring Coatham was proposed. Attempts at a compromise by having one pier at a central point between the two resorts failed, as each town wanted the structure on their stretch of seafront, so the planned building of the rival piers commenced.

The building of Redcar Pier was financed by the selling of shares, with the Earl of Zetland, Lord of the Manor of Marske, making a generous donation. J.E. & A.Dowson of London had designed the pier some years earlier (J.E. Dowson had built several piers in the 1860's but he died in 1868) and Head Wrightson & Co. of Stockton, who had completed Scarborough pier just down the coast, were engaged to construct it.

Admiral Chaloner of Guisborough drove in the first pile in August 1871, and the pier was officially opened two years later on Whit Monday 2nd June, 1873. The complete length of the pier was 1,300 ft, and it was twenty feet wide, at the entrance, where three minaret kiosks were located, which housed the toll collectors office, ladies and gentlemen's rooms, and a shop. A bandstand complete with sheltered seating for 700 people was erected on the 114 ft wide pierhead. There was also a separate landing stage, available at all periods of the tide, for passengers using the pleasure steamers which ran to Middlesbrough, Saltburn and Whitby. The pier is generally thought to have cost £11,000 to build, though another local source at the time of its opening quoted £6,250 as the cost.

Redcar Pier, like all of its neighbours on the Yorkshire coast, was to suffer a stream of serious misfortunes, mainly caused by the severe storms which sometimes hit this stretch of coast. At the end of October, 1880, the brig 'Luna' driven by a severe storm (which also damaged Hornsea and Withernsea Piers, further down the coast) cut through the pier, and repairs cost the pier company £1,000. On New Year's Eve 1885, the S.S. 'Cochrane' ran against the pier and demolished the landing stage. The Redcar Pier Company was unable to arrange for this to be repaired and there were no longer any facilities at the pier to enable steamers to call.

Further damage occurred to the pier on the 12th January, 1897, when the wreckage from the abandoned storm-damaged Norwegian Schooner 'Amarant' was driven through the pier, causing a breach twenty yards wide. This was repaired in the summer of 1897, but the following summer saw the pierhead burned down on the 20th August, 1898. It was believed the fire was caused by an unextinguished wax vesta falling between the planks. The repair bill was between £1,000 and £1,500 and this included the rebuilding of the sheltered seating, albeit on a less grand scale. The bandstand, however, was not rebuilt and this was replaced by a mobile bandstand on the promenade which was trundled between the rival resorts of Redcar and Coatham for alternate band concerts.

In 1907, a pavilion housing a large ballroom was constructed at the shoreward end of the pier. It was extended, to include a café, towards the shore in 1928 and the original entrance kiosks were re-roofed and absorbed into the frontage of the ballroom.

The pier, like many on the south and east coasts of England, was breached in 1940 to prevent it being used by the enemy in the case of invasion. During the war, a mine exploded near the pier, considerably weakening the already decaying structure, and eventually the majority of the pier was washed away in succeeding storms. At the end of the war, only the pier pavilion and some 45 ft of neck beyond it remained.

The Redcar Pier Company was wound up in 1946, and the pier was sold to Redcar Borough Council who spent £4,500 on the purchase and restoration of the remnants of the pier.

During the east coast storms of January, 1953, the pier pavilion and cast-iron legs of the pier were both damaged by exceptionally high tides. Repairs were made and the smallest seaside pier in England continued to provide entertainment to residents and visitors alike. Danny Mitchell and his Music Makers were the resident orchestra in the pier pavilion for a number of years. A Wurlitzer Organ was installed in the ballroom in 1979, and a series of celebrity concerts proved to be very popular. These last days of the pier's life were said by some to have been amongst the best.

In 1980 the pier was declared unsafe and closed. Major structural repairs were needed to the cast-iron legs and Langbaurgh Borough Council, who owned the pier, were unable to justify the expense of the repairs, and they decided that the pier must be demolished. An offer to buy and remove the pier for £250 was accepted by the Council, and work started a few days before Christmas 1980. The pavilion and decking were removed within four weeks and the site was finally cleared by March 1981.

This left Saltburn as the only surviving pier on the Yorkshire coast.

Left: Redcar Pier in 1896 with the original bandstand and sheltered seating on the pierhead. These were later destroyed by fire on 28th August 1898.

Below: Redcar Pier in 1899, shortly after the pierhead had been badly damaged by fire.

The Pier, Redcar

Left: The fire-damaged pierhead of Redcar Pier waits to be reconstructed c1900. An interesting array of amusement machines and articles for sale can be seen at the pier entrance.

Below: The sheltered seating on the pierhead of Redcar Pier was rebuilt in the early 1900s, but the bandstand was not replaced, though a mobile version was used on the promenade.

4237.4 Rough Sea at Redcar Pier

Above: The underdeck ironwork on Redcar Pier was particularly attractive. Similar ironwork still survives on Cleethorpes Pier, which was also built by Head Wrightson.

Right: Redcar Esplanade around the turn of the century. The three minaret kiosks at the pier entrance were quite distinctive and contained a shop and ladies and gentlemen's rooms.

Above: Redcar Pier c1910 showing the pavilion at the shore end, which had been built in 1907.

Right: The Pavilion of Redcar Pier was extended towards the Promenade in 1928 and two of the entrance kiosks were re-roofed to blend in with the pavilion.

THE PIER, REDCAR. 10049.

Left: A dilapidated looking Redcar Pier, possibly sometime during the Second World War. The pavilion end of the pier seems to be having some repairs done, while the end of the pier seems to have disappeared altogether.

Below: Storms and an exploding mine combined to wash away the majority of Redcar Pier during the Second World War. This view from just after the war shows that only the pavilion and a small stump of pier-neck survived.

Redcar Pier in the mid 1950s, now the smallest seaside pleasure pier in Great Britain. The pavilion continued to be a popular venue for concerts and other forms of entertainment until the pier's demolition in 1981.

COATHAM PIER:1875

During the 1860's, the twin towns of Redcar and Coatham were developing into rival seaside resorts. In 1866, the Redcar Pier Company was formed to build a 'Promenade and Landing Pier', but nothing was done until a rival scheme for Coatham was proposed in 1870. An attempt to build one pier to serve both towns failed, as both Redcar and Coatham wanted the structure on their particular stretch of coast, and so the rival piers were constructed.

Work started on building Coatham Pier in 1873, on the sea-front opposite Newcomen Street (now Station Road). The length of the pier was planned to be an ambitious 2,000 ft, 700 ft longer than the rival pier at Redcar which had been built between 1871 and 1873. By December 1874, the pier was nearing completion, but disaster struck when the brig 'Griffen' and the schooner 'Corrymbus' were driven through the pier during a bad storm. The 'Griffen' went through the centre of the pier, eventually getting stuck on the beach. All of its crew managed to survive by jumping onto the pier as the vessel crashed through it. The 'Corrymbus' breached the pier nearer the promenade, but unlike the 'Griffen' it was a total loss. The cost of repairing the pier was high, and the proposed length of 2000 ft, was reduced to 1,800 ft, to help reduce the overall cost of construction.

Coatham Pier was finally opened in 1875, and it was a fairly impressive structure containing two pavilions, one in the centre of the pier and the other just inside the entrance. The latter housed a roller-skating rink whilst the former, which was mainly of a glass-plated construction, was a hall for band concerts.

During its short and sad life of only twenty-five years, Coatham Pier was only moderately successful and it was frequently damaged by storms. Its fate was effectively sealed on the 22nd October, 1898, when it was cut in two by the storm-damaged Finnish barque 'Birger'. Several thousand spectators from both Coatham and Redcar had gathered on the promenade to witness the 'Birger' break up in heavy seas, killing all but three of its crew of fifteen. The surviving three men had managed to cling onto a piece of wreckage, and as it passed under Coatham Pier, ropes were lowered to haul them to safety. One of them managed to scramble onto the pier, but another fell back into the sea to his death. The third man was washed up onto the beach where he was revived. Those people who had gathered on Coatham Pier to watch this sad spectacle then had to run for their lives as the wrecked 'Birger' came towards the pier. Eventually it crashed through the structure near the glass-plated pavilion causing a breach a hundred yards wide, before coming to rest on the beach.

The Coatham Pier Company, already in severe financial trouble due to the costs of earlier repairs, were unable to meet the crippling repair bill needed to restore the pier, and they demolished the isolated seaward section. In the following year (1899), the pier company crashed, and the rest of the pier was allowed to deteriorate until it was eventually dismantled for scrap.

The entrance kiosks and roller-skating rink, which were built on the promenade not on the pier structure itself, survived into the new century. The pavilion housing the roller-skating rink was demolished in 1910, to be replaced by a glass shelter called the 'Glasshouse' which incorporated the kiosks. In 1928 the 'Glasshouse' was rebuilt as a theatre/cinema called the 'New Pavilion', and the kiosks disappeared along with the last traces of Coatham Pier, one of the most obscure of all Britain's seaside piers.

Left: Coatham Pier was severed by two storm damaged vessels on December 9th 1874, whilst nearing completion. One of the vessels, "Griffen" lies stranded on the beach, shortly after the disaster.

Below: A rare photograph of Coatham Pier, sometime in the late nineteenth century. The two entrance kiosks were unusually built of brick, though the left hand kiosk seems to be boarded up and out of use.

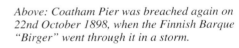

Above: Coatham Pier was breached again on 22nd October 1898, when the Finnish Barque "Birger" went through it in a storm.

Left: The severed pierhead and pavilion of Coatham Pier shortly before their demolition in the winter of 1898/99.

Left: The glass-plated pavilion of Coatham Pier, shortly before its demolition in 1898/99. The Coatham Pier Company went bankrupt and the remainder of the pier was demolished by the end of the century.

Below: The rival stretch of esplanade between Coatham and Redcar Piers in 1899. Coatham Pier can just be seen, awaiting its final demolition.

The Esplanade, Redcar

RELIABLE SERIES.

Left: The entrance kiosks and roller-skating pavilion of the former Coatham Pier c1905.

Below: The Regent Cinema, built in 1928 as the New Pavilion stands on the foundations of Coatham Pier.

WITHERNSEA PIER: 1878

The two small hamlets of Withernsea and Owthorne on the Holderness coast of Yorkshire joined the ranks of the Victorian "Watering Places" with the coming of the railway from Hull in 1854. Alderman Anthony Bannister, Mayor of Hull in 1852 and brainchild of the railway, had ambitious plans to turn Withernsea into a major seaside resort, and in 1871 he formed the, "Withernsea Pier, Promenade, Gas and General Improvement Company". The following year saw the company issue their prospectus and plans for the new Withernsea, which included a pleasure pier sited in the north of the town. A design was drawn up for this pier, but the idea was soon abandoned in favour of a new pier, sited opposite the railway station. Work began on this pier in 1875 with Thomas Cargill as the engineer (his only other pier venture was the short-lived uncompleted pier at Aldeburgh in Suffolk) and J. O. Gardiner as the contractors.

During its construction, the pier suffered some storm damage, but the work was completed by August 1877, and in the following year, it was officially opened to the public after having cost £12,000 to build. The appearance of the pier was deemed most "pleasing", with the timber decking and iron girders being supported by delicate cast-iron piles which were screwed into the beach. Seating was provided along the whole of the pier's 1,196ft length and a saloon was built on the pierhead. Admission to the pier was a penny.

At the pier entrance, a large brick-built castellated gateway (supposedly modelled on Conway Castle) was erected and this was soon affectionately nicknamed "The Sandcastle". To ensure stability, the foundations of the gateway were embedded in the clay, and to enable maintenance to be carried out without the need for further excavation, Cargill had a tunnel dug beneath them which ran below the pier to an exit door on the beach.

For its first two years the pier was fairly successful, especially with the large number of day-trippers from nearby Hull. The pier company even made a small profit, but disaster loomed just around the corner.

On the 28th October 1880, a fierce storm raging along the Yorkshire coast caused untold damage to the county's piers. Redcar and Hornsea Piers were badly damaged by ship collision, and Withernsea Pier was hit by two different storm damaged vessels. The "Jabez" hit the end of the pier and sank with all hands while the coal barge "Saffron" punched a 200ft hole through the middle of the pier and came to rest on a nearby groyne. Her crew sat out the storm until morning, and then lowered a rope ladder and walked to safety. The "Saffron" had been one of a fleet of ships which set out from their shelter of the Humber during a lull in the bad weather to continue their journey northwards. Around eight o'clock the vessel was near Flamborough Head, when suddenly the wind increased to storm force, unleashing the fury of the sea. The Captain of the "Saffron" decided to head back towards the Humber, but the wind ripped away all the sails, and with torrential rain making visibility impossible, the vessel was left to the mercy of the wind and the sea. She was helplessly driven southwards along the coast until she crashed into Withernsea Pier around one o'clock in the morning.

The pier was repaired using timber instead of iron, but further damage occurred on the 28th March 1882, when a stormy sea washed away the the pierhead and its saloon. This time the pier was not repaired, but it continued to be used for several more years, despite being repeatedly damaged by storms.

Withernsea never did become a major seaside resort, though it continued to grow in size throughout the late 19th Century. Unfortunately its major showpiece, the pier, received another deadly blow during the night of the 20th October 1890 when the Grimsby fishing smack "Genesta" hit it during the storm. This vessel had run aground at nearby Waxholme on the previous evening with the loss of the captain's life, but it emerged from the ordeal relatively unscathed, and on the following day a group of local businessmen acquired it at an auction. They hardly had time to admire their new investment before another storm drove the unmanned "Genesta" along the coast to Withernsea until it crashed into the pier. More than half of the pier was completely destroyed, and with just 300ft of it now remaining, it was beginning to look a sorry sight indeed.

At the inquest on the "Genesta's" captain, the coroner doubted if the tragedy would have occurred if a guiding light had been located at Withernsea. As a result of his findings, the building of the lighthouse was started in 1891 and on the 1st March 1894 it shone its first beam out over the North Sea.

Alas for poor old Withernsea Pier, the lighthouse arrived one year too late. On the 22nd March 1893, the pier was effectively destroyed when the storm damaged steel vessel "Henry Parr" (formerly "Dido") crashed into it at high speed, sending a shower of sparks over the many spectators on the promenade who had ventured out on the bright moonlit night to witness the goings on.

All that remained of the pier was a mere 50ft, which survived until 1903 when it was removed during reconstruction work on the sea wall. Two of the cast-iron support piles remained imbedded in the beach for a short time until they were removed as well.

The pier's name lived on, however, in the castellated twin towered gateway at the pier entrance, which still survives today. They are generally known as the "Pier Towers" or "Pier Head" (a confusing term as the pierhead normally refers to the seaward end of a pier), and they have been used for a number of different purposes and activities over the years. Soon after the pier's demolition, the north tower became the Beach Master's office, while the south tower became a penny bazaar and gift shop. Pierrot shows often used them as a backdrop, and in the 1950s, the south tower became home to a coastguard station.

Along with the now closed lighthouse, the Pier Towers are probably the most distinctive and well known landmark in Withernsea, and they were certainly unique amongst the entrance buildings of the seaside pleasure piers of Great Britain.

Today they still provide a convenient rendezvous for holidaymakers and residents alike, who arrange to meet at the "Castle".

Left: Withernsea Pier in 1877, nearing final completion. The pierhead acquired a saloon shortly after this photograph was taken and the pier was opened to the public in the summer of 1878.

Below: The "Saffron" lies stranded on the beach, after smashing a 200ft hole through the centre of Withernsea Pier during the great storm of 28th October 1880.

Left: The grave of the four crewmen of the "Jabez", the second ship which hit Withernsea Pier during the storm of the 28th October 1880. Three of them are buried in St Nicholas Churchyard, Withernsea and the other one at nearby Holmpton.

Below: Withernsea Pier, shortly after having been repaired, following the "Saffron" disaster. The gap in the pier was rebuilt, with wood rather than cast iron, but in March 1882, the pierhead and saloon were washed away by a stormy sea.

*Above: The last 50ft of Withernsea Pier
waits to be demolished c1897. Ship
collisions in 1890 and 1893 had almost
totally destroyed the pier.*

*Right: Withernsea Pier entrance c1900.
Anyone receiving this postcard could be
forgiven for thinking that Withernsea
boasted a fair sized pier. Little did they
realise the pier ended just out of shot!*

Withernsea Pier was demolished in 1903, leaving only the pier towers and two of the supporting piles remaining. The latter were removed sometime during the Edwardian Period.

Above: The entrance towers of the former Withernsea Pier in 1905. The left hand tower housed the Beachmaster's office, whilst the right hand tower was used as a gift shop.

Left: The Pier Towers Withernsea during the 1920/30s. A tea bar now stands on the beach, where long ago, the graceful pier strode out to sea.

Left: The Pier Towers stand isolated on Withernsea seafront, sometime during the 1920/30s.

Below: Withernsea Pier Towers in the late 1980s. The hut on the right hand tower was erected in the 1950s, when the coastguard station was sited there.

HORNSEA PIER: 1880

The quiet seaside town of Hornsea became a "watering place" in the late eighteenth century with the discovery of three chalybeate springs of health-giving water. A regular coach service to Hull was started in 1821, and the Hull and Hornsea Railway arrived in March 1864.

The man behind the building of the railway to Hornsea, local man Joseph Armitage Wade, next planned to build a promenade pier for the budding resort. He formed the Hornsea Pier Company in 1865, and in the following year he obtained a Board of Trade order to build the pier, which was to lapse if the pier was not built within five years. By 1871 no pier had been built (though some ten piles had been sunk which were eventually washed away), but in 1873 Mr Wade renewed his option and formed a new pier company which proposed to build a pier 100 yards south of the railway station.

Unfortunately for Mr Wade, another local businessman, Mr Pierre Henri du Gillon of Leeds, had bought some land in nearby Hornsea Burton and he planned to build a pier and harbour some 700 yards from Mr Wade's site. Conflict between the two men was inevitable when it was discovered access to Mr du Gillon's pier from the railway station would be over land owned by Mr Wade, and a violent disagreement ensued between the two men.

In 1876, Mr du Gillon's Hornsea Pier, Promenade and General Improvement Company obtained a Board of Trade order to construct their pier, which was now due to be part of a whole new town drawn up by Mr du Gillon and his architect. A tramway was planned to run from the railway station on to the end of the proposed 818 yard pier. Mr du Gillon's plans, however, seemed to be a bit over ambitious, as events were soon to prove.

In June 1877, the legal contest between the rival pier companies came before the House of Commons Legal Committee, who eventually passed both pier bills! For a short time, it seemed Hornsea, a small town of just 1,600 souls, would acquire two piers, but in April 1879 Mr du Gillon's Company was declared bankrupt due to the cost of litigation between the two pier companies, and it was wound up. Mr Wade, who seems not to have been a very likable character, gloatingly wrote a letter of triumph to the Hornsea Gazette.

Work finally began on constructing Mr Wade's pier in the summer of 1878 with Messrs G. Bergheim & Co as the Contractors. The prolific pier engineer, Eugenius Birch, famous for his piers at Brighton, Eastbourne and Blackpool amongst others, designed the pier, but Hornsea was to be his least successful structure.

Unfortunately, the pier company had only managed to raise a small capital of £8,700 to build the pier, and by the summer of 1879, both contractors and Birch were petitioning for the liquidation of the company in order that they could be paid. Bergheim stopped all work on the pier, and eventually another firm of Contractors, Messrs De Fontaine & Co, finished constructing it.

In May 1880 the 1072ft long pier was finally opened, fourteen years after the pier company had first been formed. The AGM of that year, however, revealed no profits for the Company due to it owing over £2,500 to the contractors, and the pier went into the hands of the official receiver.

Nevertheless, the opening of the pier proved a great attraction in the little resort, which had little else to offer the erstwhile visitor at the time, but its active life was to be a very short one.

On the night of the 28th October 1880 a terrific storm raged along the Yorkshire coast causing numerous ships to be wrecked. Withernsea and Redcar piers were both damaged by ship collision, but Hornsea pier fared worst, losing its 92ft long pierhead and 120ft of the rest of the structure when the "Earl of Derby" hit the end of the pier.

Virtually the whole town had rushed out on to the beach to see this sad spectacle. The lifeboat could not be launched as the horses to pull it were unable to face the severe winds and heavy rain, and the lifeboat crew had to watch helplessly as many other stricken vessels could be seen foundering in the huge waves. Amazingly the crew of the "Earl of Derby" all survived, but those of some of the other vessels were not so lucky. Because of the near pitch darkness, the pier attendant had not realised the end of the pier had been destroyed until he was crawling along the pier to put the pierhead light out and suddenly found one of his hands was in an open space where the pier should have been.

Mr Frank Hobson, who has lived in Hornsea all of his life, recalls that his grandfather was in the lifeboat crew and after the collision, he ran along the pier with his lamp to see what had happened. Apparently some of the crew members of the "Earl of Derby" were coloured men and as they clambered onto the pier, Mr Hobson's grandfather, never having seen a coloured person before, ran for his life thinking the devil was after him!

What Mr Wade thought of this destruction after fifteen years of constant hassle in getting the pier built was not recorded for posterity.

Unfortunately this was the end of the road for Mr Wade and the Hornsea Pier Company, and though they remained in existence for some years to pay off outstanding debts, the remaining 750ft of the pier was allowed to badly deteriorate at the hands of heavy seas and storms. The pier was reported derelict in 1897, and most of it was removed in 1910 when the promenade was reconstructed. A few remains survived until 1929, when they were blown up as they had proved hazardous to local shipping.

One of the seats which once adorned the pier deck still survives to this day, as does the pier company's brass commemorative plaque which was rescued from a scrap timber yard in 1965. Some of the pier's wooden beams and iron stanchions were excavated from the pier site some years ago and they can also be seen.

Hornsea Pier may be long gone, but it is certainly not forgotten in the picturesque little resort. The 1991 Hornsea information brochure entitled "Lakeland by the Sea" informed its readers that over sixty years ago, Hornsea once boasted a pier.

Above: Hornsea Pier in the summer of 1880, soon after it was officially opened to the public.

Left: A Victorian gentleman surveys the wrecked Hornsea Pier, after "The Earl of Derby" had demolished the seaward end during a storm on 28th October 1880.

Above: Hornsea Pier c1890. Now 750ft long, following the "Earl of Derby" disaster. The protracted litigation between the pier and ship owners prevented the pier from ever being used by the public again.

Right: Hornsea Pier in the 1890s, slowly rotting away into oblivion. By the turn of the century, the pier was derelict and the majority of it was removed c1910.

The former entrance buildings of Hornsea Pier survived in use as an amusement arcade until they were demolished in the late 1920s.

Surviving fragments of Hornsea Pier. The seat (above) was once part of the continuous seating which lined both sides of the pier deck. The wooden beam (right) once supported the pier decking.

APPENDIX: CHRONOLOGICAL INFORMATION TABLE

PIER	BUILT	ENGINEER	CONTRACTOR	ORIGINAL LENGTH (FT)	DEMOLISHED	OWNERS
Scarborough (N)	1866-69	E. Birch	JE Dowson (1866-68) Head Wrightson (1868-69)	1000	1905	Scarborough Prom. Pier Co. Ltd (1869-1889). North Pier Co. (1889-1904) William Morgan (1904-1905)
Saltburn	1868-69	J. Anderson	J. Anderson	1500		Saltburn Pier Co. (1869-1883) Owners of the Middlesbrough Estates (incorporating the Saltburn Estates) (1883–1938) Saltburn and Marske UDC (1938-1974) Langbaurgh Borough Council (1974-)
Redcar	1871-73	JE & A Dowson	Head Wrightson	1300	1981	Redcar Pier Co. (1873-1946) Redcar Borough Co. (1946-1968) Teeside Borough Co. (1968-1974) Langbaurgh Borough Co. (1974-1981)
Coatham	1873-75	N/K	N/K	1800	1899	Coatham Pier Co. (1875-1899)
Withernsea	1875-78	T. Cargill	J. Gardiner	1196	1903	Withernsea Pier, Promenade Gas & General Improvement Co. (1878-1903)
Hornsea	1878-80	E. Birch	Bergheim (1878-79) De Fontaine & Co (1879-80)	1072	c1910	Hornsea Pier Co. (1880-c1910)

SELECTED BIBLIOGRAPHY UP TO 1992

Further reading on the Seaside Pleasure Piers of Yorkshire and Seaside Piers in general can be found in the following publications:-

ADAMSON Simon — Seaside Piers (Published by B.T. Batsford 1977)

BAINBRIDGE Cyril — Pavilions on the Sea (Published by Robert Hale Ltd 1986)

BAINBRIDGE Norman — Saltburn-by-the-Sea (Published by Sotheran, Redcar 1977)

BAINBRIDGE Norman — Saltburn-by-the-Sea in Old Picture Postcards (Published by the European Library 1985)

COCKROFT Janet — Redcar & Coatham: A History to the End of World War II (Published by Sotheran, Redcar 1976)

COOKSON David — Triumph & Disaster - Three Humberside Piers (Article in "Bulletin" - Humberside College of Higher Education news for Staff and Students No 55 - January 1986).

COOKSON David — Seaside Resorts in Humberside (Published by Hull College of Further Education 1987)

COOKSON David — The Story of Withernsea Pier (Article in "Around the Wolds" magazine - Summer 1990)

FISCHER Richard & WALTON John — British Piers (Published by Thames and Hudson 1987)

HOBSON Jean — A Sketch of Hornsea (1974)

MELLOR G.J. — The Lost Piers of Yorkshire (Article in "Dalesman" magazine Vol. 26 1964)

MICKLEBURGH T. — The Guide To British Piers - Second Edition (Published by the Piers Information Bureau 1988)

MILLS P. — The Pier That Was (Article in "Yorkshire Life Illustrated")

SCOTT WILSON Chris — The History of Saltburn (Published by Seaside Books 1983)

SOTHERAN Peter — The End of the Pier Book (Published by Sotheran Redcar 1981)

SOUTHWELL G.L. — Hornsea in Old Picture Postcards (Published by the European Library 1983)

WHITEHEAD John — Withernsea: A Popular History of a Popular East Yorkshire Seaside Resort (Published by Highgate Publications 1988)

WHITTAKER Jack — Withernsea in Old Picture Postcards (Published by the European Library 1985)

WHITTAKER Jack — Old Withernsea and Surrounding Villages Remembered (Published by Hutton Press Ltd 1990)